"Three tofts to Mainard the Fleming"

Site of the St Andrews Mint? *See page 17*.

# The Coins of ST ANDREWS

by

Veronica Smart

with illustrations by
Christine M Wolfe

---oOo---

*"To God and to St Androis he
Grantit the stryking of the money ...."*

---oOo---

St Andrews University Library

1991

Published by St Andrews University Library,
North St., St Andrews, Fife, KY16 9TR.
Printed by St Andrews University Printing Department.



**British Library Cataloguing in Publication Data**

Smart, Veronica
The Coins of St Andrews
I. Title
737.4941292

ISBN 0-900897-09-0

*Cover design, Christine M Wolfe,*
*see Chapter III*

*Contents*



*The following text has been omitted from the bottom of page 29:*

After the death of James III, all the coins of the realm were struck in Edinburgh, with the exception of an issue of base metal bawbees for Mary, which was struck in Stirling.

## *Foreword*

It comes as something of a surprise to many people, even to those St Andrews residents who are interested and well-informed about their city's history, that St Andrews once boasted a mint and that coins still exist which bear its name. Unlike castle, colleges and cathedral, there is no building to which we can confidently take our visitors or put up a plaque saying 'On this spot stood the Mint of St Andrews', though there are some clues as to where it may have been. Nevertheless, the mint was one of the oldest institutions of the burgh and the inscriptions on its little products constitute some of its earliest documents.

The reason for this obscurity lies doubtless in the historical and numismatic problems which surround its existence. The pennies have to tell their own story, since the greater part of the mint's history took place in a period from which few documents survive to explain the Scottish coinage, and they cannot be expected to speak out unequivocally. Nonetheless, the unravelling of the tale of the St Andrews mint is not without its own interest. This little book is intended to relate what we know of the mint in terms interesting and intelligible to the non-specialist, and to bring this shadowy monument of the St Andrews past to the acquaintance of resident and visitor alike.

St John's House
ST ANDREWS

January 1991

Chapter I

# *Coins in Scotland before David I*

Scotland was one of the last nations of Europe to have a coinage of its own. Before the Romans arrived in Britain many of the Iron Age tribes such as the Iceni who lived in East Anglia and the Coritani whose territory was in and around Lincolnshire were striking coins. At one time it was thought that the powerful Brigantes tribe of northern England did so too, but it is now accepted that Ancient British coinage was never minted north of the Humber.

During the time when Britain was part of the Roman empire, coinage from all the imperial mints circulated freely, and Roman coins have been found in Britain emanating from Antioch, Lyons, Cordova, Alexandria - in fact from all over the Empire - as well as from Rome itself. For most of the period none was actually made in Britain, though mints in London and Colchester worked briefly during the reigns of Carausius and Allectus, and the mint at London worked for Constantine and his successors in the early fourth century.

Many Roman coins have been found in Scotland, on native sites like the hill-fort of Traprain Law as well as in association with Roman forts and camps.

Although present-day national boundaries had of course not then been established, the territories of Europe which had been longest and most firmly integrated in the Empire - roughly, Italy, France and Spain - continued to strike coins without any hiatus for their new barbarian kings. The continental Germanic tribes, including the Angles and Saxons who settled in England, began to strike coinages in the sixth and seventh centuries AD. The earliest English coins are dated to around 640.

By the year 1000, the Vikings from Scandinavia had made themselves very familiar with other peoples' money and had begun to mint their own in their homelands. Vikings who had travelled eastwards to become princes in Kiev produced the first coinage in Russia since Greek outposts on the Black Sea centuries earlier, by imitating Byzantine gold pieces in their own names round about the end of the tenth century. The earliest Irish coinage was part of this same movement, since the Viking colony at Dublin struck silver pennies from about 995 onwards. It has recently been suggested that the colonists of the Isle of Man were minting similar pennies at the same time.

One surviving coin bears the name of the illustrious Welsh prince Hywel Dda, King of Dyfed, who died in 950. This piece has the same design as the pennies of his English contemporary King Eadred, and has on its reverse the name of Gyllis, who was one of King Eadred's Chester moneyers. Although no mint-name appears on this coin it is very much in the Chester style, and most numismatists would conclude that it was struck there rather than in Wales, and for ceremonial or diplomatic rather than economic reasons. Otherwise, Wales had to wait for the establishment of a mint by William the Conquerer at Rhuddlan, and possibly at Cardiff and St Davids.

Meanwhile, it would not be true to say that coinage was unknown in Scotland, though all the evidence suggests that the Picts and Scots themselves in these centuries did not have much use for coined money in an economy based on self-sufficiency and barter.

The frontier between England and Scotland fluctuated and was often ill-defined, so the few finds south of the Forth and Clyde are really an extension of the use of coinage in the kingdom of Northumbria. A large hoard of ninth-centry Northumbrian copper coins was found at Paisley in 1787, and finds of Northumbrian coins have been made at

Jedburgh and the Glenluce Sands in Wigtonshire. At Cockburnspath a considerable find of King Athelstan's pennies was made in the mid 19th century. At the lake-dwelling site Buston Crannog in Ayrshire two fragile gold shells, the remains of plating on a copper core, were found in 1880. This is a surprising find, since coins of that design, imitating the forerunners of the English silver coinage, and dating from the early seventh century, are extremely rare even in England. How it got there, and how it was regarded by the crannog dwellers, is a puzzle.

The current excavations at Whithorn have proved exciting numismatically as well as in other ways. The coins are likely to have been brought there by pilgrims to St Ninian's Candida Casa, and thus are not evidence for monetary activity in the area generally. Predictably, Northumbrian coppers have been found there, but less predictably, a silver penny of Beonna, an eighth century king of East Anglia, and one of the Dublin Norsemen of c. 1035.

Most of the Scottish coin-hoards, however, from the tenth century to the beginning of Scotland's own coinage in the twelfth, are the result of the activities of the Vikings. They are quite unlike English finds of the same period, which bear out the effectiveness of the laws of the English kings in prohibiting the circulation of foreign coin in the territory under their control. Viking treasures contain a mix of coins from many sources, English, continental and even oriental, combined with silver ingots, ornaments, arm-rings and suchlike, hacked up into small pieces, which constituted part of the currency of the Vikings before the Scandinavians began to strike their own coins. This silver was traded by weight, coined and uncoined, unlike in a true monetary economy where a coin carries a pledge of value not directly dependent on its content of precious metal.

As well as in Orkney and Shetland, such Viking hoards have been found in North Uist, Trotternish in Skye, Inchkenneth off Mull, Tiree, Iona and Islay. On Colonsay and Arran, English coins were found in Viking burials. From Argyll southwards, there are a few finds from the fringes of the mainland. In the east of Scotland finds from this period are rare. That the Moray Firth must have been a scene of Viking activity is testified by a small tenth-century treasure from Tarbat, a coin of King Alfred from Burghead and two of slightly earlier Mercian and West-Saxon kings from Croy.

Few early mediaeval coins have been found between the Moray Firth and the Forth. According to the New Statistical Account of 1845 an exotic find was made in the churchyard of Monymusk in Aberdeenshire, of an Arabic dirhem from Morocco. Arabic coins often occur in hoards of Viking treasure, but seldom as late as this one, which is dated to AD 1098.

Nearer home, in Fife, at Parkhill Farm, Lindores near Newburgh, near the shore of the Firth of Tay, an interesting but now rather enigmatic find was made in 1814. The coins have now all been dispersed, but fortunately before this happened the find was shown to the minister of Abernethy, Andrew Small, an enthusiastic if somewhat naive antiquary. Small wrote a book entitled Interesting Roman Antiquities, but into it he threw something of everything, including some hilarious place-name interpretations. Though far from knowledgeable about mediaeval numismatics, his descriptions are vivid and leave no room for doubt that what he saw were coins of King Canute, of his second issue on which the king is unusually depicted wearing not the crown or classical diadem but the pointed Viking-style helmet with nose-guard - 'like the Pope's turban' Small says. (Plate 1) What else the hoard contained is very uncertain, but if, as has been suggested, there were continental deniers, the find-spot would support Viking activity in the Tay.

St Andrews University Library houses three silver pennies all of Canute's last issue, but their provenance is unknown.

*Actual size*

*Plate 1*: 'Like the Pope's turban'. *Pointed Helmet* type of coins of Canute, c. 1025, similar to those found at Lindores, Fife.

It is unlikely that a coin-collector would acquire three coins of the same type if these were not from a hoard, and the strong supposition must be that this was a local find. The University's Swallowgate archaeological museum contained a tiny 'cut halfpenny' of Edward the Confessor; the Anglo-Saxons seldom minted round halfpennies and farthings and the method of making change for their silver pennies was literally to shear them into halves and quarters. This piece was reputedly found on Tentsmuir. Perth Museum has a group of Edward the Confessor coins from the middle to the end of his reign which may be from a Scottish hoard, again of unknown provenance; if so, this must be the latest Scottish coin-find before the beginning of the Scottish coinage. There are no finds of coins of William the Conqueror or William Rufus from Scotland.

One would expect that if towns and trade were evolving in Scotland in the late tenth and early eleventh centuries, then the volume of coins found for the same period would have increased, but this is not the case. Up to the foundation of the burghs, coinage seems to have made a minimal impact on life in Scotland.

Chapter II

# *David I and the Beginnings of the Scottish Coinage*

When David I acceded to the Scottish throne in 1124 he was already middle-aged and had spent much of his early life in England. His sister Matilda was the queen of Henry I; his wife, another Matilda, was the daughter of Waltheof, Earl of Northumbria, and through her David had obtained the earldom of Northampton and the Honour of Huntingdon. William of Malmesbury, the English chronicler, wrote (with that superior tone that has not been lacking since) that David became "polished from a boy with familiarity with us". For good or ill, David returned first to Lothian which he inherited on his brother Edgar's death and then to the whole kingdom of the Scots full of admiration for the Anglo-Norman institutions he had witnessed, and ready to implement them on his own ground.

A great deal has been written about the feudalisation of Scotland and the introduction of English and Normans by King David in its pursuit. There is, too, an ongoing controversy over the founding of the burghs; whether they were entirely new, or whether in some cases David was able to adapt small but already existing urban communities and markets to the model with which he had been acquainted in England. However that may be, one important feature of the English borough was its right to strike coins.

This is a strange concept to us, used as we are to a unified coinage from one source, the Royal Mint. The Norman conquerers had left behind in France a poor and ill-organised system of coinage, and inheriting a sophisticated and efficient monetary economy from their Anglo-Saxon predecessors, they had wisely let well alone, particularly as the English system of frequent recoinages brought repeated remuneration to the Treasury. There was no displacement of the Anglo-Saxon officials who ran the mints in the boroughs; we know this because one of the methods of control was the obligation of the moneyer to place his name and that of the mint as the reverse inscription of the coin, and the same names that sign Edward the Confessor's pennies appear on those of the Conqueror, continuing over many issues. Only very gradually do Norman-French names take over, and this has more to do with changes in fashion in christening children than with changes in the nationality of the personnel.

At the time when David was living in England and administering his English counties, most of the English boroughs had moneyers striking coins. Both Northampton and Huntingdon were minting towns (Plate 2). Thus in David's mind coinage was inextricably linked with the burghs, a component of their *raison d'etre,* trading and exchange.

Early mediaeval coinage is not dated; James V was the first Scottish monarch to place the date on his coins in 1539. Proper financial records from the earliest period are almost non-existent. However, we can date the beginning of the Scottish coinage to about 1136 with some confidence. We are helped by the fact that new coinages tended to be imitative of the old and respected; for example, the Scandinavians in their homelands and in their Irish colony copied the English pennies which were the common currency of northern Europe. So with the earliest Scottish coins, copying the still revered English silver penny or 'sterling' although, as we shall see, it had declined severely in striking and workmanship from the standard of its Anglo-Saxon ancestor.

The earliest English issue imitated in David's name is the last type of Henry I's reign. As has already been mentioned, the English coin types were changed frequently, and this type

*Actual size*

*Plate 2:* Silver penny of Henry I struck at Huntingdon, one of David I's English possessions.

would not have been struck much before 1134. Henry I died in 1135 but this coin, crucial to the history of the Scottish coinage, carries the mint-signature of Carlisle, which was not in Scottish hands until early in 1136.

Henry I's only son had died in the disaster of the sinking of the White Ship, and his heir was his daughter Matilda, to whom he had made his barons swear allegiance. On Henry's death, however, her cousin Stephen began to press his claim to the throne, which resulted in the so-called Anarchy or civil war which was only finally resolved by the accession of Matilda's son as Henry II in 1154. Since Matilda was David I's niece he supported her claim or at any rate the crisis gave him a valid excuse to invade England in 1136 and seize Carlisle. Thus although this 'first Scottish' coin bears the designs of Henry I, it was certainly struck after Henry's death, but before new designs had reached Carlisle.

Carlisle was a new mint that had been set up by Henry about 1130 to coin silver from the Cumbrian mines. Its possession would have provided David with a convenient starting-point for the introduction of coinage into his realm, since he would have found a ready-equipped workshop and an experienced master moneyer to hand. Indeed, the same moneyer Erebald went on very soon afterwards to strike coins at Edinburgh which imitate Stephen's earliest issue. Later, Roxburgh, Berwick and Perth joined David's tally of mints, still imitating English pennies.

As the Stephen versus Matilda conflict proceeded, the English coinage echoed the political anarchy, breaking down into any number of regional issues as the supporters of the rival parties gained victories or suffered defeats, all issuing their own designs, some with facing or profile heads, standing or mounted figures, with all kinds of heraldic crosses on the reverse.

Towards the end of his reign, probably in the late 1140s, David standardised his coinage by bringing in a new design which was all his own. The obverse retained the profile portrait which came from the English coins but the reverse was original: a bold cross fleury (that is, a cross with each arm terminating in a fleur-de-lis), usually with a pellet in each angle. As with the English coinage, the reverse legend consisted of the moneyer's name followed by the name of the mint. It was at this phase of the coinage that St Andrews enters the story.

Chapter III

# *Mainard, Provost and Moneyer*

The story of the find of the beginning of the St Andrews mint is a fascinating one, and depends not on any new archaeological find but on the piecing together of already known fragments of evidence to recognise their significance.

Although the fifteenth century chronicler Andrew of Wyntoun described Alexander III confirming the right to strike coins to the Bishop of St Andrews, a right going back much further than his own reign, until a few years ago all the coin-catalogues and works of reference listed St Andrews as one of the mints that only opened in the time of Alexander III. No coins bearing the town's name earlier than this reign had been discovered, and there was a feeling that Wyntoun was perhaps repeating a mere poetic formula, or wished to give his own priory the prestige of more ancient rights.

It has already been mentioned how the standard of workmanship in the English coinage had deteriorated very badly by the end of the reign of Henry I, and under Stephen it became even worse. The dies themselves were often crude and ill-cut, and poor striking technique failed to transfer the image clearly on to the blank. The coins were struck by placing the blank piece of silver between the upper and lower dies and striking the resulting sandwich with a heavy hammer-blow. The Anglo-Saxons and early Normans seem to have used some kind of collar to maintain alignment, but this seems to have been omitted in many later examples so that slippage occurs, some of the inscription falls off the edge of the coin and the opposite edge is compensatingly blank. Thus the English issues of the 1140s were sorry godparents to the infant Scottish coinage, and the imitations did nothing to improve on the prototypes.

Again, although the moneyer's name is spelled out in full, the abbreviation of the mint-name was always dependent on the amount of space that remained. Some of the surviving specimens of David's reign (which are far from plentiful) have quite indecipherable mint-signatures and form a sub-group which defeats attempts to attribute them to any known mint. The coins which have proved to be from St Andrews had previously been assigned to this group.

In the early 1980s an English collector bought from one of the smaller coin-dealers a silver penny which bore the portrait and design of David I's last issue but legends which he could not decipher. He enlisted the help of Dr I H Stewart, the author of the standard work on the Scottish coinage and of major articles on the early Scottish mints, to ask if he knew of any other coins struck from the same dies as his purchase, which might preserve details worn away or lost in striking, and thus supply an attribution.

From Dr Stewart's own collection, from a coin in the British Museum and from plates in an old auction catalogue, no fewer than seven coins emerged, all linked by being struck from combinations of two obverse and three reverse dies.

Where the obverse legend is clearest, it appears as NAVIT REX, which must be a mistake for DAVIT, the usual form of the king's name on coins of this type. The clearest reverse reads +2 MENAVD: SAN, another +MENARD.I.SA: or +MEINARD.I.SA:, and on the third only SAN is plainly legible, with a V as fifth or sixth letter - that is, in a similar position to the MENAVD die. (Plate 3). The interpretation of the 2 symbol is very uncertain. It seems most likely that Menard or Meinard, and Menaud are intended as the same name; although they are originally of separate derivation, Meinard from Meginhard ('strength' + 'hard') and Menaud from Meginvald ('strength' + 'rule') such a confusion of elements is far from unknown at this period. The name is neither Gaelic nor English, but

*Actual size*

*Plate 3*: One of the first coins of St Andrews: silver penny struck by Mainard c. 1050.

Continental Germanic, a term which takes in the Frankish names of France and the Low German of the Netherlands, and would allow the bearer to be a Norman or a Fleming.

Here the coins begin to tie in with our earliest knowledge of the history of the burgh. A seat of the foremost bishopric of Scotland since the time of King Constantine, and a place of pilgrimage to the relics of the Apostle, St Andrews was an important settlement before David I licenced the founding of the burgh. There is no early foundation charter still surviving, but in the sixteenth century Thomas Mutto, the then Town Clerk, assembled the documents in the town's Charter Chest and in the resulting compilation, the so-called Black Book of St Andrews, there occurs a copy of a confirmation of a grant of three tofts of land in the burgh from Bishop Robert (1126-59) to one Mainard the Fleming, because he was among the first to build up and equip the burgh, founded by Bishop Robert with the licence of the king. Maynard is described as having been formerly the king's own burgess in Berwick, and as Bishop Robert's *praefectus* in St Andrews.

Although we know the burghs to have been settled by incomers, Normans, Englishmen and immigrants from the Low Countries who were famous as merchants and traders, it would seem very unlikely that in the little emerging burgh there could have been two Mainards holding important official appointments under the Bishop at the same time. Mainard is sometimes credited with having been the first 'provost' of St Andrews but it is important to remember that his appointment derived from the Bishop, his feudal superior, and not from election or representation of his fellow-burgesses, and similarly his first responsibility was to the Bishop. In the terminology appropriate to the time, he is perhaps better described as the Bishop's reeve, or as we would say, steward and magistrate.

It was exciting, therefore, to find Mainard's name on the coinage of St Andrews, but not surprising to find him carrying out this duty for his ecclesiastical master. Episcopal as well as royal coinages are a feature of the Middle Ages. In Anglo-Saxon times the archbishops of Canterbury of the ninth century not only had their own moneyers, but placed their own names and a coped and tonsured effigy in place of the diademed image of the king upon their pennies. The eighth and ninth century archbishops of York similarly struck coins in their own names, but later, as we know from records, bishops and abbots had their own moneyers, from whose output they drew a revenue, although their coins are distinguished only by some minor mark, or are totally indistinguishable from the royal money. We know from later records (see below) that St Andrews followed this pattern and in the earliest days too the coins must surely have been struck on the bishop's behalf, since St Andrews was the bishop's burgh, and Mainard his servant.

It would be satisfying to be able to point to some spot in the town and say 'Here stood the Mint of St Andrews' but its location is very uncertain. There are two possibilities. Because of the need for security for the dies, it has been suggested that mediaeval mints were housed where possible in a castle. The so-called 'cunzie hous' in Stirling Castle was held to support this view, but this building is no longer considered to have had anything to do with minting. Such documentary evidence as exists seems to point to the 'mint' being the moneyer's workshop in the same way as a tanner, potter or goldsmith carried on his business on the street floor of his dwelling, living on the upper floors with his family and apprentices. An intensive study of Winchester, for which surveys of property exist for the eleventh and twelfth centuries, bears out this view, and Cochran-Patrick in his 'Records of the Coinage of Scotland' cites several examples of houses in burghs being used as places where the coinage was struck.

It would be reasonable, then, to look for Mainard's mint in a house that he would build on one of the three tofts granted to him by Bishop Robert.

The declaration in the Black Book of St Andrews states that the three tofts granted to Mainard ran *a vico burgendi usque ad rivum prioris* : 'from the burgh street down to the prior's stream'. The prior's stream must mean either the Lade or the Kinness Burn, and thus the likelihood is that the three rigs in question ran down to it from the south side of the present-day South Street. Since we know that the building up of South Street proceeded westwards from the priory, and since the same declaration describes Mainard as being among the first to build in the burgh, he must have built well towards the east end of the street. If we accept the identification of the mint with a house built on Mainard's rigs, it probably fronted on to South Street in the vincinity of Abbey Street. (see frontispiece).

Chapter IV

# *From Malcolm IV to Alexander III*

David I died in 1153. His son Earl Henry died before him, and he was succeeded by his grandson Malcolm IV. Malcolm was only twelve at the time of his accession and died when he was twenty-four. Coins in Malcolm's name are extremely rare. It was not infrequent in mediaeval times for posthumous coinages to continue to be struck after the death of a king; for example, the only known coin of Richard I of England is a modern forgery, the real coins of his reign, and for that of his brother John, being pieces struck in the name of his predecessor Henry II. It seems very possible that many of the coins of David I's last issue, in which the St Andrews mint appeared, were in fact struck in Malcolm's reign.

What is much stranger is that no St Andrews coins are known for Malcolm's brother William who succeeded him as William I, generally known as William the Lion. The volume of coinage struck in Scotland seems to have been growing and William's coinage is comparatively plentiful. The dating of William's early issues is provided by changes in the English coinage which the Scots continued to follow, but his third coinage, a Short Cross issue (i.e. with the cross on the reverse reaching only to the inner circle and not to the edge of the coin) can be firmly dated by an entry in the Chronicle of Melrose to 1195. This states that in this year William King of the Scots reformed (*innovavit*) the coinage. In the new issue there are a number of coins which bear the names of two or more moneyers and hence have no room for a mint-signature. It is thought that these moneyers were working in partnership with each other, and that they were maybe itinerant and struck coins for different towns. However, in the angles of the short cross are figures known heraldically as 'mullets' - stars, sometimes hollow, but with a varying number of points.

It seems likely that the number of points may be a kind of code to indicate the mint of issue, in place of the mint-signature. A later issue, in the reign of Alexander III, which has **both** mint names and varying-pointed mullets, may supply the key to break the code. In such a scheme, the combination for St Andrews would be those coins which have two mullets of five and two of six points. (Plate 4).

This phase of the coinage is very perplexing. Not only do moneyers who are known earlier for different mints now appear to be working jointly, such as Hue of Edinburgh and Walter of Perth, but the reverses with different mullet patterns appear on coins which use the same obverse die. We cannot be certain what, if anything, was going on by way of minting in St Andrews at this point. Perhaps the town was visited by a travelling moneyer who struck coins for the bishop during his stay and then moved on, but perhaps the only new coins were those struck elsewhere.

William I was succeeded by his son Alexander II but it is not until the next reign, that of Alexander III, that the mint of St Andrews emerges again from obscurity. Within a year of his accession, Alexander III undertook a major reconstruction of the Scottish coinage. At the beginning of the reign it seems that most of the minting activity had shrunk to the border towns of Roxburgh and Berwick. Roxburgh has completely disappeared now as a town, but the survival of its name in county and parliamentary constituency is a reminder of its earlier importance. It was a favoured resort of Alexander II, the place of his marriage to Mary de Coucy in 1239 and was the birthplace of Alexander III.

In 1250, the *Scotichronicon* tells us, the Scottish coinage was renewed, so that the cross on the penny which formerly

*Actual size*

*Plate 4*: Penny of King William the Lion, moneyer Henri le Rus, possibly struck at St Andrews c. 1195.

did not cross the circle now reached to the outermost edges. This change had taken place in England the previous year. It is thought that this change was accompanied by the decision to recall all the coinage then in circulation and reissue in the new type. This would partly explain why previous issues are so scarce, since only pieces already lost or hoarded would survive the exchangers and the melting-pot. It seems likely too that the new coinage meant an increase in the production and use of coin, and a large number of new mints were opened and earlier mints re-opened at this time. Perth, Edinburgh, Aberdeen and with them St Andrews, were re-opened, and a number of towns appear for the first (and in many cases the last) time: Ayr, Dumfries or perhaps Dunfermline, Forfar, Glasgow, Inverness, Kinghorn, Lanark, Montrose, Renfrew and Stirling.

The name of St Andrews appears at greatest length on a coin reading ANDER; so much of the mint-name is achieved by the ingenuity of the die-cutter in saving space by using the arms of the Long Cross as the uprights of his Ms and Ns. On other dies it reaches only to AN, but this abbreviation is linked firmly to St Andrews by the name of the moneyer, Thomas or Tomas, who strikes coins with no other town's name. (Plate 5). Unlike his predecessor Mainard, we know nothing about Thomas except for his name on the coin. In England we know that the office of moneyer was often passed down in families, but whether Thomas was a descendant of Mainard's, or whether he held any other office in the burgh we cannot tell. Being the Bishop's moneyer, even in this fairly prolific phase of the coinage, can scarcely have been a full-time job.

In 1280 another change took place in the coinage. Whatever its usefulness in the monetary affairs of the time, it means bad news for local historians; the mint-name disappears again, since the king's titles are extended to ALEXANDER DEI GRA/REX SCOTTORVM, continuing in the reverse

*Actual size*

*Plate 5*: Penny of Alexander III struck by Thomas (THOMAS ON ANDER); type struck 1251-80.

legend where the mint name formerly had its place.(Plate 6). As has been mentioned above, the system of differing patterns of mullets continues, but now we are on rather firmer ground than was the case previously when it was conjectured that this system may have denoted the locality on whose behalf the coins were struck. For the later Alexander III coins we have independent corroboration that coins were still being struck for the Bishop of St Andrews although the burgh name is wanting.

Proper mint-accounts are still wanting, but occasional references do occur in chronicles, as we have seen, which enable us to check our deductions from the material survivals. The verse chronicle of Andrew of Wyntoun was not written until the early fifteenth century, but as a canon of St Andrews priory Wyntoun undoubtedly had access to earlier traditions and probably written manuscripts for his information. Under the year 1283, he tells how Alexander III travelled to St Andrews from Lindores where his son Alexander had recently died. Whilst he was here, he confirmed to Bishop William Fraser the right of striking coins:-

Alexandere oure king
That Scotland had in governyng
Came in till his ryalte = his royal posessions
Till Sanctandrois the cite
And standand in the kirk rycht there = standing
Devotly forouth the hie altere = in front of
In presens of all that stude by
He grantit and gaif there frely
To God and to St Androis he
Grantit the stryking of the money
As frely and as fulely
As ony bischop before gane by
In thare times had sic thyng
In his time, or his faders the king, = or of the king his father

*Actual size*

*Plate 6*: Penny of Alexander III, 'Rex Scotorum' reverse without mint-name, but showing the St Andrews figuration of 2 stars of five points, 2 of six. After 1280.

Sauffand the declaration = except for
Off the superscription
And the feftment of that thing = granting
To remane ay with the king.

Wyntoun probably intends us to imagine a grand public occasion: 'in presens of all that stude by', since if only the bishop's household and the king's retainers were witnesses, the incident might as well have been set in the bishop's palace. There were several churches within the precinct wall at this time, St Mary on the Rock and others dedicated to St Peter and St Leonard, as well as the original parish church, but given the importance of the meeting between the king and the bishop, we are probably meant to understand the Cathedral itself, and envisage Alexander standing at its high altar.

We are not told much about the practicalities, though it is made clear that the 'feftment' - the power of granting or licence - was always to be at the king's discretion. It could not be claimed as an independent right if at any time the king wished it to be discontinued. If the previous couplet, on the superscription, is also dependent on this, it means that the king would give orders and it was not up to the bishop to choose what he would put on the coins. It might, of course, be contrasting the new pennies without the name of the city with the old money of bishops gone by who could name St Andrews. It is unlikely that Wyntoun meant his readers to understand by this that the king was forbidding the bishop to put his own name and title on the coins, though this practise was not unknown on the continent.

Wyntoun here states categorically that the bishops of St Andrews struck coins, or at least had the right to do so, in the time of the king's father Alexander II. Having only fairly recently seen St Andrews recognised as a David I mint, we should not be too hasty in dismissing this claim, and may hope one day to see it confirmed, whether by the discovery of new coins, or by the reattribution of known pieces.

Alexander III's reign saw the innovation of round halfpennies and farthings, bringing to an end the old practice of cutting silver pennies in half to make small change. This took place as part of the 1280 recoinage; similar provision had ocurred in England the previous year. Occasional issues of round halfpence had been known earlier, but from now onwards they were a standard denomination of the coinage.

Chapter V

# *Balliol and Bruce*

The long reign of Alexander III had been a time of peace and prosperity, during which trade and the burghs flourished, as is well exemplified by the increase in volume of the coinage and the growth in number of towns named as mints. His death at the cliffs of Kinghorn in 1286 signaled the beginning of years of turmoil, during which rival claimants strove for the crown and fought off the predations of the English King Edwards who sought to exploit the situation in their own claim to overlordship.

William Fraser, the Bishop of St Andrews whom we saw confirmed in his minting rights by Alexander III, was from the very beginning of the conflict a strong partisan of John Balliol. Whilst the death in Orkney of Margaret the Maid of Norway, Alexander III's only direct heir, on her way to Scotland was still only a rumour, Fraser was writing to Edward I to enlist his help in avoiding civil war, and putting forward Balliol's interest. It is scarcely surprising then that Fraser should have struck coins at St Andrews styling him King John - Iohannes Dei Gra. (Plate 7). Other coins go on to finish the title on the reverse with Rex Scotorum, but St Andrews was the only burgh whose coins bear a mint-signature, and this - Civitas S Andree - takes up the whole of the space available for the reverse legend. Apart from St Andrews we are unable to tell which other mints struck coins for John, though it is thought that Berwick was the main one. By the time John abdicated in 1296 he had lost Berwick, Edinburgh, Roxburgh and Stirling to the English.

John Balliol's coinage falls into two groups, the 'rough' and the 'smooth'. The former and earlier is poorly engraved and struck and has a grainy surface; the latter is finely produced. Halfpennies are known of both kinds, but St Andrews halfpennies are very rare.

*Actual size*

*Plate 7*: Penny of John Baliol, 1292-96, with St Andrews inscription CIVITAS S ANDRE.

Coin-hoards show that Alexander III sterlings continued to circulate in far greater numbers than the John coins, and it is possible that some centres may have continued to strike coins in Alexander's name posthumously. This is unlikely to have happened at St Andrews, where the products of the mint in John's name are so clearly identifiable, and where the mint's proprietor is known to have declared for John.

William Lamberton, Fraser's successor to the see of St Andrews, was a stalwart of the opposing camp. In 1299, the year after his consecration, he was invovled in the quarrel between Bruce and Comyn at Peebles, and was already marked as a Bruce supporter. He was present at the coronation of Robert I at Scone by Isabella Buchan in 1306, and his friendship was rewarded by the presence of the king at the consecration of his newly completed cathedral in 1318. Nevertheless, when Edward I, then virtually in control of all lowland Scotland, called a parliament at St Andrews in 1304, Edward confirmed and restored to Lamberton all the temporalities of his see. It might seem doubly surprising then that minting at St Andrews seems to have ceased with the end of Balliol's coinage.

It is, however, generally believed that minting ceased altogether in Scotland betwen 1296 when Berwick was lost and 1320 when it was recovered, after Edward II had failed to hold his father's conquests. Robert I's coinage is rare, and probably confined to Berwick. Thereafter, great changes took place. His son and successor David II took part in the movement which ended the centuries-old monopoly of the silver penny with the introduction of a bi-metallic system of denominations: gold noble (1/3 of a pound); groat (four pence), pennies, halfpennies and farthings in silver. Gradually, Edinburgh achieved prominence, though there were issues from Dundee under Robert II, Berwick, Inverness, Stirling and Linlithgow under the Jameses, and a more constant output from Aberdeen and Perth. After the death of James III, all the

## *Interlude - Dumbarton Groats*

In the opening years of the fifteenth century a curious incident occurs, which though it did not take place in the city was certainly connected with the bishopric, and may have concerned the bishop's right of coinage.

Bishop Walter Trail died in St Andrews Castle in 1401. The man elected to be his successor was the archdeacon, Thomas Stewart, an illegitimate son of the king, Robert II, and also dean of Dunkeld and a canon of Brechin. However, before the decree could be transmitted to the Pope, Stewart withdrew from the election, and in his place a certain Master Walter Danielston, parson of Kincardine O'Neil, was preferred to the see in his place.

Wyntoun's Chronicle fills in the story in more detail. According to his narration, the renunciation of Thomas Stewart and Danielston's elevation were engineered by the Duke of Albany. Danielston's family were hereditary keepers of Dumbarton Castle, and on the death of Sir Robert Danielston in 1397 Walter, fearing the castle might pass into the hands of one of the king's relatives, seized the castle and refused to give it up. In negotiation with the Regent Albany he eventually consented to render the castle in exchange for the Bishopric of St Andrews, a deal to which Albany was able to persuade his brother to agree.

This story's place in the history of the Scottish coinage consists of the fact that the only time Dumbarton figures in it is shortly after 1400 when groats were struck with the reverse legend VILLA DUNBERTAN. (Plate 8). They are of a quite different style from the Edinburgh groats of the same period. There is no other known reason why Dumbarton should have suddenly boasted a mint at this time, just when Danielston was aspiring to the bishopric whose temporalities included the right of minting. Possibly the groats were struck to celebrate his episcopate; if so, he had little enough to celebrate, for he enjoyed his see for only six months, and died before the year was out.

*Actual size*

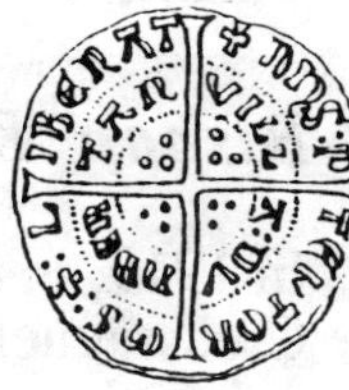

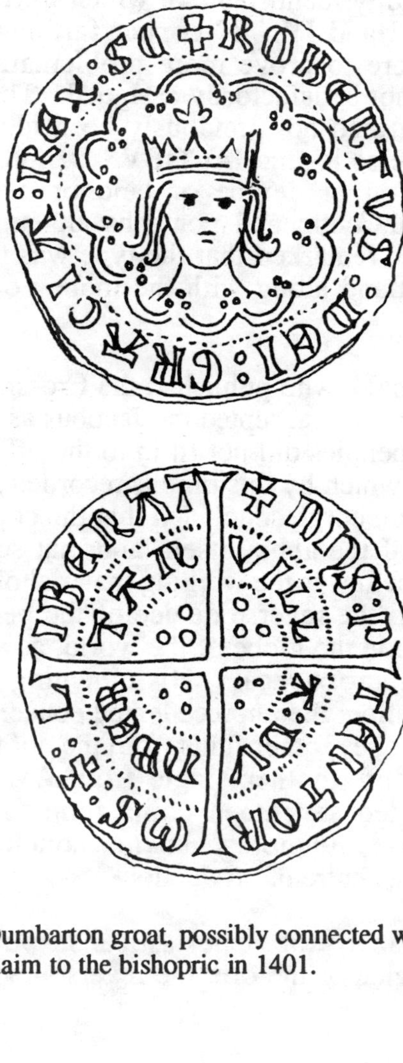

*Plate 8*: Dumbarton groat, possibly connected with Walter Danielston's claim to the bishopric in 1401.

Chapter VI

# *Bishop Kennedy's Coinage*

In 1919, in a drain that had formerly flushed the latrines of Crossraguel Abbey in Ayrshire, a find was made of 205 coins, the most readily identifiable of which were from the reigns of James III and IV. 87 copper farthings and 51 copper pennies were to prove more problematical. The farthings are still not satisfactorily assigned. The pennies were of a type that had not previously been identified as Scottish. The obverse legend IACOBVS DEI GRA REX, with no designation or device of land or people was applicable to several Continental monarchs, although as early as 1862 it had been remarked that the type was frequently discovered in Scotland along with the money of Scottish kings.

Sir George Macdonald, who published the Crossraguel find shortly after its discovery accepted the Jacobus as a Scottish King James. The pennies did not fit in to the official royal coinage, however, which by this time is recorded in Acts of Parliament, and Sir George concluded that the copper coins were the product of the abbey itself, and that some scrap metal found with them was the working material of the mint. He thus interpreted the reverse device of the pennies, the orb, or cross set upon the globe of the world, as a rebus on the abbey's name: 'cross regal'. His clinching argument was that of distribution: the unprecedented concentration of these coins at the abbey, other finds from the not far distant Glenluce Sands, and another single from Ayrshire. In fairness he recorded seventeen coins found in eastern Scotland, but these did not shake his conclusion that Crossraguel was the centre of production.

The pennies are clearly of ecclesiastical inspiration. In addition to the device of the orb, the reverse legend is the opening line of an evening hymn by Prudentius: CRUX PELLIT OMNE CRIMEN 'the cross dispels all harm'. In 1950 Robert Stevenson challenged the attribution of the coins to a remote and obscure Ayrshire abbey, for which no royal warrant for minting had ever been known. By then, more examples had been discovered and plotted on the distribution-map, which began to show a clear bias away from the South-West, towards Fife and South-Eastern Scotland.

Four of these so-called Crossraguel pennies had been found in 1860 on the Kirkhill in St Andrews, and in searching for a locus which would fit both the ecclesiastical context and the new distribution, St Andrews began to appear as a strong candidate. In the first place, the ancient minting-rights of the bishops has been explicitly renewed in favour of Bishop Kennedy by James II, in a charter of 1452. Then, the orb device, as many St Andreans will recognise, is closely associated with Bishop Kennedy. Although not from his personal coat of arms, it was the principal feature of the arms of the college of St Salvator which he founded, and several items testify to the antiquity of this blazon. It appears still on a shield on the college mace, on a stall-end and a bell originally from the college, as well as from pieces of college plate which have now vanished.

Although this suggestion for the pennies from the Crossraguel find was not made in modern times until 1950, there is a much earlier account which attributes this coin-type to the episcopal mint of James Kennedy. In 1683 George Martine, a local antiquary, in writing about the coinage rights of the bishops of St Andrews, observes:

"For proofe that this priviledge was sometime in use I have seen copper coins bearing the same mond chapletted and adorned with a croce, just as in all things the mond set by Bishop Kennedy in sundrey places in St Salvator's College both in stone and timber, and in this way adorned". Martine goes on to add that some coins of this type were preserved in the charter-chest of St Andrews Town Council in his own day. (Plate 9).

The evidence for these copper pennies with the device of the orb being the product of James Kennedy's right to mint coins as Bishop of St Andrews seems on the whole very convincing, though the attribution has not achieved universal acceptance. It has been objected that there are features of the lettering which are not paralleled on the regular coinage until the 1470s, far too late for Kennedy associations. Another objection has been that, calculating the volume of the coinage from the different varieties of design and the number of dies employed on the known examples, it was too extensive to be merely an episcopal emission. This opinion perhaps does not take into full consideration Kennedy's political importance; as minister of the crown and guardian of the young king James III, his power spread beyond his ecclesiastical domain. In a recent letter, Mr Stevenson stated that his opinion is still very strongly in favour of a Kennedy connection for these pennies, though he concedes that the issue may have been long-lived and have continued to be struck after Kennedy's death. And we may ask, since James II particularly mentioned the Bishop of St Andrews' privilege of striking his own coins in the charter to his friend and counsellor, which as far as we can tell had been in disuse for over a century and a half, where else are we to look for the exercising of that privilege?

Mr Kenneth Fraser has recently pointed out to me that certain gold coins of the Holy Roman Empire from c. 1410 to the middle of the century carried a representation of the imperial orb. The Crux Pellit pennies, if they are Kennedy's, would seem to have had a different inspiration, i.e. Kennedy's devotion to the symbol of the Holy Saviour, and his use of the device in the context of his college almost certainly pre-dates his coinage. Also, the representation of the orb on the Scottish coins is more naturalistic and does not copy the geometric German device; however, the German coins, if known to Kennedy , may have suggested that the symbol was not inappropriate as a coin type.

*Actual size*

*Plate 9*: 'The same mond chapletted and adorned with a croce'. Pennies attributed to Bishop James Kennedy (1440-66).

## *Postscript*

With the end of the Kennedy coinage the story of a St Andrews mint comes to an end. And indeed, in 1709 the story of the Scottish coinage itself came to an end, swallowed up by the Royal Mint in London, in spite of the fact that the Lords Commissioners for Scotland had consented to the unification of the coinages only on condition that a mint be guaranteed to Edinburgh in perpetuity. Certain issues of coin - in old shillings, and new pound coins - have been struck for Scotland with differentiated designs by the unified mint, and our banknotes continue to fly an old banner.

The numismatic history of Scotland also continued in a minor way into the nineteenth century, and St Andrews features here too. In the eighteenth century up till, and beyond, the issue of copper small denominations in 1797 under George III, many private concerns issued their own tokens for use as small change, which was otherwise scarce. Local tokens are interesting items for collectors as many are pictorial, showing local landmarks or allusions to local legends, or illustrate the trade of the issuer. These tokens obviously had a function of advertising the business of the issuer, but there are other pieces which had no commercial function other than advertising, but were made as counters for cards or children's games.

If any St Andrews tokens of either kind exist, they must be extremely rare. There are, for instance, none listed for St Andrews in Dalton and Hamer's *Provincial Token Coinage*, but the author has had one piece described to her as being issued by an Alexander Colville, in business in South Street as a grocer in the early nineteenth century. If any reader should know the whereabouts of an example of this token, or indeed of any tokens or counters of St Andrews tradesmen, she would be grateful if they would communicate the information.

In addition to these trade tokens, the various churches in Scotland also issued tokens, as a certification of fitness of their members, after successful catechising, to attend Communion. A relic of this practice still survives in the pasteboard cards given out by elders before a communion, though nowadays these have the nature of an invitation rather than a means of discipline.

According to O. D. Cresswell, who published a directory of communion tokens in 1985, these tokens flourished most in times of religious dissension when it was important for members of different (and often violently opposed) congregations to be able to recognise their own people. Thus the Disruption of 1843 brought new life to a practice which Cresswell observed as beginning to flag. The earliest tokens, often square but also in a variety of shapes, are locally made and have a homely charm, made usually of lead or lead alloy which is easy to work, but notoriously bad for conservation. These are mostly made by pouring into moulds rather than striking cold metal. Their devices tend to simplicity and brevity: the abbreviated parish name, the minister's initials, and the date at most. Later examples, which were commercially die-stamped, gave the opportunity of greater elaboration, and here we find the texts of the Institution and exhortation - the favourites 'This do in Remembrance of Me', and 'Let a man examine himself' but a wide variety of others.

The Kirk Session minutes of Holy Trinity, many of which are deposited in the University Muniments, supply details of early tokens and give an interesting insight into their production.

These entries make it clear that the earliest recorded tokens for Holy Trinity must have been made not from metal but written on paper. On October 2nd 1651 the Session paid for 2 'quares', i.e. eight double folio sheets, of 'lumbard' paper, 'to write tokens upon'. Twelve years later, however, it was agreed that 'Patrick Gardine goldsmith shall have thirteen shillings and fourpence for each hundred of six hundred tickets he made at their desire'. The mention of Gardine's profession here suggests that the 'tickets' were now being made of metal, and subsequent entries confirm this. In 1668 Gardine was paid for a further 700 'tickets' and in 1681 it was reported to the Session that Patrick Gardine was leaving St Andrews, and that the two stamps which he had for stamping the tokens were to be given to William Greig, hammerman, (a term describing any kind of smith) and Gardine was to teach Greig how to strike the tokens before he left the town.

The earliest surviving metal token for a St Andrews church appears somewhat later, in 1722, for Holy Trinity though it has no other identification than ST AND and the date. One of 1753 has ST AND in monogram and the initials MIB (Mr James Bennet) but no token is known to cataloguers between this and one dated simply ST ANDWS 1818. A much more elaborate Town Kirk token, undated but probably mid nineteenth century, has an obverse of St Andrew on his cross as on the arms of the city, with the Burning Bush and its motto Nec Tamen Consumebatur ('but it was not consumed') the badge of the Church of Scotland, on the reverse. (Plate 10).

The parish church of St Leonard issued a token in 1780, identified by the letter L for the parish name, and the minister's initials MRW for Mr Robert Watson. Another was issued in 1831 with the name of the church spelt out in full.

That the Free Church took the name of Martyrs from its beginning is made clear by its token of 1843. Its inscriptions are Free Church of Scotland Martyrs Church, and the texts 'Let a man examine himself' and 'Lovest thou Me?'. The Associate Congregation, the result of an earlier secession from the Established Church, later to become a

United Presbyterian congregation and then to reunite with the Church of Scotland as Hope Park Church, is represented by an undated token reading ST ANDREWS UNITED ASSOTE CONGREGAN, with the text (with the overtones of a dig at the Established Church?) The Lord knoweth them that are his.

Again, if members of any of these churches know of any tokens that are not included in the above lists, they are better placed than outside numismatists and cataloguers to come by such knowledge, and the information would be gratefully received.

*Actual size*

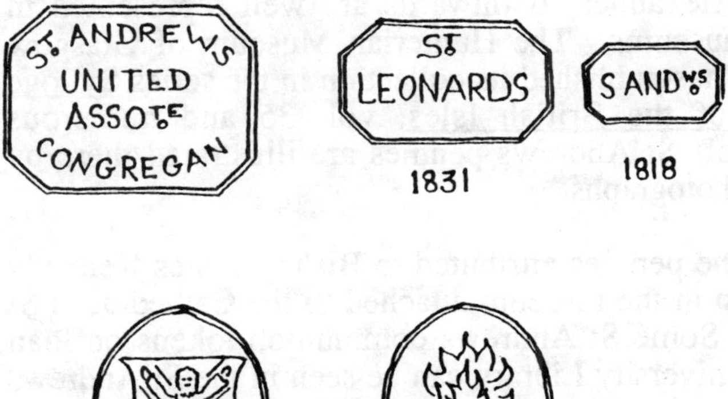


*Plate 10*: A selection of St Andrews communion tokens.

## *Notes, some locations, and reference for further reading*

Since the coins discussed here were originally struck in low relief and have since suffered wear and damage, it was thought that illustration by line drawing would give the reader a better notion of their design and inscriptions than would photography.

The ideal is to see the coins themselves. The earliest pennies (Chapter III page 13) are great rarities and apart from one example in the British Museum are all in private hands. At the time of publication one example is on loan to the St Andrews Museum in Kinburn House. Also to be seen there are two pennies of Thomas's issue for Alexander III and two John Baliol CIVITAS S ANDREE pieces.

Coins of Alexander III onwards are well represented in Scottish museums. The Hunterian Museum of Glasgow University has published its collection in the series Sylloge of Coins of the British Isles, vol. 35 and numerous examples of St Andrews pennies are illustrated there by excellent photographs.

A few of the pennies attributed to Bishop James Kennedy can be seen in the museum attached to the Cathedral in St Andrews. Some St Andrews communion tokens on loan from the University Library can be seen in the St Andrews museum.

The Mainard pennies from the foundation of the borough are illustrated and described by J. E. L. Murray and Ian Stewart in vol. 53 of the British Numismatic Journal, for 1983. The Kennedy pennies are discussed by R. B. K. Stevenson in vol. 84 of Proceedings of the Society of Antiquaries of Scotland. The standard work on the Scottish coinage is I. H. Stewart's, The Scottish Coinage, revised edition 1967, published by Spink & Son of London. This is supplemented by an article 'Scottish Mints' in a collection of essays Mints Dies and Currency, ed. R. A. G. Carson, published by Methuen, London, 1971.

The coin-dealers B. A. Seaby Ltd publish a well illustrated Standard Catalogue of Scottish coins, giving current prices for collectors, which is updated from time to time. A fascinating source-book for the period when documentary evidence is available is R. Cochran-Patrick's Records of the Coinage of Scotland, published in 1876.

The early hoards from the Viking period (Chapter I page ) are described and mapped by R. B. K. Stevenson in Sylloge of the Coins of the British Isles, vol 6, and later hoards are listed in British Archaeological Reports 45, Coinage in Mediaeval Scotland, which contains much of background interest though not specific to St Andrews.

I am greatly indebted to Mr R N Smart, Keeper of University Muniments, for the details of striking tokens from the Holy Trinity records, hitherto unpublished. Also to Dr R G Cant for his observations on the possible location of the St Andrews mint.